AMERICAN HELLSCAPE

*What you can do now to save the world
and rebuild thriving communities*

Douglas Vogel

To Willis

CONTENTS

A LONG ROAD AHEAD

INTRODUCTION

History repeats itself, first as tragedy, second as farce

KARL MARX

"They had a bunch of tugs trying to pull and push it earlier but it was going nowhere," Jilianne Cona wrote on Instagram on March 23rd, 2021. She was referring to the Ever Given, an ultra-large container ship which lodged itself sideways in the Suez canal, causing more than one billion dollars in losses across diverse industries and economies.

At just over thirteen hundred feet long, the *Ever Given* was one of the largest ships in the world, and its colossal accident gripped the world's collective attention and imagination for nearly a week as engineers, military personnel, and mariners sought to refloat it and reopen the canal for navigation.

"For decades shipping has been the invisible conveyor belt at sea, enabling large manufacturing industries like automotive to do just-in-time shipments, even though from time to time shippers are calling foul in terms of the reliability of the schedule," an analyst for Lloyds told *The Guardian* at the time. "Some production lines may be halted due to containers being caught in traffic like this." The *Ever Given* crisis came at just about the one-year mark of the COVID-19 pandemic, after a year of supply chain disruptions, labor shortages and geopolitical decisions led to shutdowns across industries and caused runs on toilet paper, meats, and packaged goods in grocers and retailers around the world.

A ship stuck in the Suez? It became a symbol of the wider crisis almost immediately, drawing into stark clarity the knife's edge upon which our global economy perches. Today, across the developed world, we rely on complex supply chains to bring us the fruits of modern life at a whim - Tide pods from Amazon Prime, a litter box from Target, a new Kia assembled in Alabama but reliant on metals, textiles, and chips from Thailand, Korea, and Africa - and we're perilously close to losing it all.

In 2022, the USDA assures Americans that "there are currently no nationwide shortages of food, although in some cases the inventory of certain foods at your grocery store might be temporarily low before stores can restock in any industry." Yet, grocery stores like Harris Teeter are cutting store hours in an effort to mitigate the effects of a dwindling workforce driven away by low pay and unreliable hours. Walmart and Giant say they're working with alternate suppliers to ensure customers have *something* to buy, and acknowledge they are having pockets of Pet food companies are having difficulty meeting demand as aluminum prices rise, threatening can production, and the number of pet-owning households grows. Produce growers face skyrocketing fertilizer prices driven by geopolitical games between American and Chinese businessmen and diplomats.

You might ask *How does it really affect me if Purina can't make as much canned food or Dole can't grow as much lettuce?* As you probably know but tried to convince yourself otherwise, everything is interconnected. Your neighbor who works in marketing? She relies on clients like Purina to make money and hire her. Your brother or sister who's making their way through college and works at a local bar? Their employers rely on brewers and food distributors to stay open.

Small businesses like brewers, farmers, bakers and restaurateurs are being forced to close their doors, settle for lower quality results, or throw away products they are unable to ship as they face difficulties getting basic components for their trade (e.g., beer cans) or run into trouble shipping out their product as trucks are in short supply (e.g., dairy farmers dumping milk). Capitalism and globalization have driven us to destroy our climate and become reliant on a fast-paced supply chain, not only for creature comforts, but for basic necessities, and even a paycheck. Nobody is unaffected. That's why everyone can relate when a Twitter user writes an affirmation to the *Ever Given*: "You are NOT too much. You are ENTITLED to take up space. If the Suez Canal doesn't have room for you, that's the Suez Canal's problem."

The *Ever Given* put our modern tragedy in the light of comedy, spawning memes which will continue to make us smile for years to come, but there is no doubt that it *is* a tragedy, a crisis of economics which will disrupt the lives of millions throughout the world in the years to come. Terrible working conditions will push families to the brink and destroy relationships, lives, and communities. Monocultures and reliance on fossil fertilizers in our food system will drive us to famine, crop loss, and disease. Rising costs for materials will make modern life that much more inaccessible to the poor. And climate change will make life hotter, harder, and drier, eliminating livable green spaces, especially for urban dwellers, people of color, and the poor, leading to political discontent and instability, mental health crises, and lower productivity and engagement in society.

In this book we'll focus on a few key crises that have come together to form the supply crisis we now face: the crisis of labor, the challenges and politics of fertilizer and big agriculture, rising demand and the price crunch around aluminum, and the ever-present cloud of climate change. Lastly, we'll ask the questions… *What can you do? Is there hope? How can you plan a life and achieve happiness?*

* * *

And before we get there, and to give you reason to keep reading, I'll say now *that there is hope* and *there are things we can do* - now and together - to make this better.

HOW POOR LABOR CONDITIONS SHAPED OUR CURRENT CRISIS

"The worst is when you work a 7-to-7 and they tell you to come back at 3 a.m. on a short turnaround," Omaha President of the Bakery, Confectionery, Tobacco Workers and Grain Millers International Union Daniel Osborn told Rolling Stone in November 2021 when interviewed about working conditions at Kellogg's Omaha factory. "You work 20, 30 days in a row and you don't know where work and your life ends and begins," he told the magazine.

News of Kellogg's mistreatment of employees made national news last year, drawing an outpouring of support from labor activists and workers around the country. The Kellogg's strike stood out, even during a year of heightened labor union activity including strikes at Mondelez and unionization efforts at Amazon and Starbucks. Workers' anger at low pay and crushing demands from employers boiled over during the pandemic, frequent lack of hazard pay and corporate disregard for COVID safety standards fanning the flames of discontent. But this isn't new. Corporations have treater workers terribly since the dawn of capitalism, and before that lords mistreated their slaves and serfs as much or more. Now, after two years of a global pandemic, however, we're facing a reckoning. People are willing to walk off the job, maybe even with the promise of something better on the horizon. A class consciousness has emerged and begun to settle, and workers are no longer willing to be an exploited backbone to a modern economy that leaves them behind.

Kellogg's is an extreme example, but toxic workspaces like the Omaha plant are commonplace, and employers actions are driving workers away from essential sectors. Today, labor shortages in transportation, manufacturing, retail, and service industries threaten the bedrock of our economy. But it didn't have to be this way.

Logistics Running On Empty

Why would a trucker agree to be away from home for three hundred days out of the year? Long hours behind the wheel wreak havoc on the eyes, the back, the arms, the gut, and the mind. And nights out on the road wreak havoc on marriages, parenthood, and community and spiritual life. Since the pandemic began in full force in March 2020 and many households rediscovered the joys of spending time with one another – perhaps the only happy byproduct of the whole crisis - the number of truck drivers in the workforce has plummeted.

"I've got more jobs than I've got drivers," a recruiter in Arkansas told Vox. Today, the American Truckers Association estimates a historic shortage of eighty thousand drivers, and predicts that number will double by 2030 as "lifestyle issues" particularly "time away from home" and infrastructure issues, notably "lack of truck parking spots" and "congestion" on highways pushes current truckers into retirement and fails to provide an attractive career path to young people. This problem persists globally, too. Industry groups have documented shortages in more than twenty countries, noting labor demand in trucking is outstripping supply by Eurasia, where twenty percent of "positions when unfilled" last year according to Vox.

There are other reasons for the decline in drivers - it's not all about a difficult lifestyle and time away from the family, or even the tolls it takes on the body. The decline of unions, which accelerated under Reagan's Republican government in the 1980s, has meant "trucker wages have been shrinking for years." In the first decade of deregulation, the Teamsters Union, the primary union for truck drivers, lost approximately twenty-five percent of its membership. Further, Pew Research reports that most American households have seen their purchasing power remain stagnant even as wages have risen since the 1970s, but truckers' wages have dropped nearly fifty percent in real purchasing power since the same time frame, a staggering decline that far outpaces losses in other sectors.

America has transitioned from a manufacturing economy to a service economy relatively quickly, and what we do make here at home is differentiated in large pockets - corn and soy in the midwest, avocados and lettuce in California, cars in Michigan and the sunbelt, computers in Texas and California - so when we need something, it has to be put on a truck. The pandemic exacerbated pressures on the trucking and logistics industries, opening a "pandora's box" according to experts interviewed by *Vox*. "All of this creates a domino effect, which makes the shortage of drivers even more salient than before." When trucking moves upwards of ten billion tons of merchandise a year and is responsible for the majority of overland freight in the United States, this matters.

Today, when you go to the grocery store and can't find cream cheese – one of the products that made headlines this past fall when it went out of stock in stores across America – it can often be tied back to the trucking and logistics industry. "Cream cheese is a fresh product, meaning that keeping a large inventory on hand isn't plausible. On top of the widespread labor shortage across industries, finding truck drivers is hitting the dairy industry particularly hard because of the extra license needed to pick up milk from farms," *Supply Chain Brain* wrote in 2021, compounding effects of heightened demand, an increase of eighteen percent in at home cream cheese consumption, and a cyber attack on one of the nation's largest dairy manufacturers.

The shortage affected at-home cream cheese buyers, yes, but it also hurt small businesses that rely on the irreplaceable staple as a core component of their offers, such as bagel shops and cheesecake bakers, including Junior's Cheesecake in New York City. It was the first time in seven decades of operation that the baker ran out of cream cheese.

And cream cheese is just one example. The downstream effects of labor shortages in logistics mean a reckoning for the entire economy. Setting aside the labor shortages in manufacturing and retail we'll cover next, or the effects of commodities pricing and the climate we'll touch on in following chapters, the truck driver shortage is a crisis in its own right. If our employers don't begin to treat these workers with the respect they deserve, we may find ourselves without enough food on the table, without enough milk in our stores, without enough screws and wires to build and repair homes, or even without enough basic medical necessities to supply our hospitals and clinics.

The only path forward is to offer higher pay, more time off, greater training and support, and a deeper commitment to lifetime employment through unions, pension plans, and robust medical benefits to truckers. Truck drivers *are* the blood carrying fresh oxygen through the arteries of American commerce. We must give them what they deserve and transition to a just, clean transportation economy, or risk sliding backward to a much darker time of economic balkanization.

Tumbleweeds On Main Street

One of the most popular posts on Reddit's *Tales from Retail* goes a little like this. A woman is working in a florist. She's going to graduate college in a few weeks, and is finishing out her stint in retail. "One day, a woman came to me for balloons for her son's second birthday party," she writes. "She had already picked up her cake."

"I can't believe this bakery," the mother mutters.

"Oh, is there something wrong?" The Redditor asks.

"Yes!" She says. "Would you *look* at this cake!"

It's a nice looking cake, our author tells us. It's decorated with icing and trains. A scrolling script says: *Happy 2nd Birthday Jackson!* Our author doesn't see anything wrong, and pauses, trying to figure it out.

"Don't you *see*?" The customer asks.

"I think it's a lovely ca–" she begins to reply.

"It's in cursive. *Why the fuck would they put it in cursive! He's two!*" The customer screams, allowing her irritation at the bakery to flow out and engulf the florist.

The Redditor suggests she go back to the bakery and ask for it to be refrosted, and goes back to her work filling the balloons. From behind her, the woman calls out:

"I can't *believe* someone is to *stupid* to think this is okay!"

Without missing a beat, our author responds: "Can your son even *read*?"

That shuts the woman up. She leaves without saying another word, red faced and cowed. But what's the moral here? That if you're abused in public your only recourse is to put it online for the community to laugh at, in some way gaining catharsis and sympathy to cover up the pain of a toxic work environment where you're treated like a device, not a human being?

Another example. On September 16th, 2021, during the late stages of the Delta Variant wave, three tourists from Texas assaulted a hostess at Carmine's Restaurant in New York City. *The New York Times* called it a "melee" and the three later pleaded not guilty in court. The fight broke out days after Mayor De Blasio instituted a new vaccination check mandate at restaurants with indoor dining. The waitress asked to see proof of vaccination, and the three tourists refused. A "melee" ensued, and Carmine's released a statement of appreciation for law enforcement and for their workers, writing that they "greatly appreciate how seriously the district attorney's office is taking this attack on our staff" and going on to say that "restaurant workers are part of our city's life-blood, and today sends a strong message that criminal acts like these will not be tolerated."

These violent actors were caught. But many more aren't, and acts of violence, intimidation, and harassment are far from rare. In retail and food service, harassment by clientele is commonplace. During the pandemic, *Eater* reports, sexual harrassment of tipped workers has increased, "a substantial portion of which were requests from male customers that female service workers remove their mask so that they could judge their looks, and, implicitly, determine their tips on that basis." Are we so surprised?

Harassment alone isn't driving workers from retail and food service. It goes deeper than that. Unpredictable hours, back-breaking labor, managers who won't allow their employees to take a seat, lean against a wall, or take a break, and part-time staffing tactics designed to deny benefits to workers all combine to form a toxic and hostile work environment across the industry. *Business Insider* puts it bluntly, and correctly, in a 2021 headline: "Retail won't tackle the labor shortage until it reverses decades of worker neglect and becomes a viable, long-term career again."

But what does that mean? Like logistics, retail and food service have not kept pace with even the barest of standards of American living, leaving their workers in the dust as corporate profits have risen year after year. *Insider* tells the history of the decline in retail succinctly:

Pre-1960s, working in retail was considered a solid, sustainable job, Marc Perrone, president of UFCW, the US' largest retail worker union, told Insider.

The wages weren't the best but they also weren't the worst, he said, and when you factored in extra benefits – overtime, bonuses, pensions, employee discounts, medical, disability, and life insurance – workers felt like the futures of them and their families were taken care of. These were attractive jobs.

This began to change in the early 1960s with the arrival of big-box stores such as Walmart and Target, whose business model was to offer low prices to customers by keeping labor costs down.

It was also the start of a shift away from full-time to part-time work. Stores realized they could hire double the workers without having to pay overtime or benefits, and could schedule employees' work around consumer demand.

Now, corporations are suffering the consequences of their actions. They struggle to find workers willing to work for low wages and unpredictable hours, all while suffering verbal and sometimes physical abuse by patrons. Frankly, however, the shortage of labor in retail is not as dire as the shortage of labor in logistics. If grocery stores have shorter hours it will mean longer lines, more difficulty for working people to get to the store, and more frustration for parents juggling schedules. But we'll make do. We'll buy clothing, order dry goods, and get tools and supplies online.

It is, however, a disaster for workers, and the loss of in-person trading and commerce and the decline of dining and available food service options is a tragedy for a social, community-oriented way of life. As we suffer under the crush of a supply chain stretched thin with a lack of truck drivers, we'll have fewer and fewer local establishments left to which to turn. Fewer businesses means fewer customers buying from logistics companies, which will mean the shrinking and retrenchment of the economy at a massive scale. Good? No. Businesses, both high and low, will have failed us and our communities and left us atomized, lonely islands. The result will be a decimation of the community topped off by high prices, higher still unemployment, and society-wide shivers of anxiety. We won't have the resources to come together and find regional solutions, and will face crises on all fronts at once. This is what we face.

Our Imperative

A clear imperative emerges. From the ground up we need new, energetic community leaders to engage in wholesome business dedicated to providing stable, life-supporting jobs. Prices will be a little bit higher, but they won't be as high as in a worst-case scenario of spiraling inflation and unemployment triggered by failing supply chains and local establishments. Employers must give workers a reason to come into work: good pay, good benefits, and a role in the community in which they can take pride. We must move *now* to reorganize supply chains locally. Small business owners can do this buy buying local at scale, generating the momentum to support local growers and manufacturers. We won't *need* as many products shipped from around the world, and the ones we do need will be easier to get at better prices. If we are to have a capitalist community, we must not forget the crucial role labor plays in social relations and community; in fact, we must strive for a capitalist-laborist community, for a community dominated by the optimization of capital is no community at all.

FOSSIL FUELED FOODS & FAMINE

In the not too distant future, we may see big problems facing city dwellers in particular in relation to sourcing fresh fruit and vegetables. As fossil fuels become scarcer and more expensive, prices for fertilizer, farm machinery running costs and transportation will rise dramatically and that will be reflected in the end product.

– MICHAEL BLOCH

Most people are surprised to learn that fertilizer makes up fifty percent of all fossil fuel energy used in industrial agriculture. Worldwide, a full one percent of fossil fuel supplies are used to make fertilizer every year. And this puts us on a dangerous and unsustainable path. For several reasons, reliance on fossil fuels for agriculture places us in a bind: first, fossil fuels are political resources, second, use of fertilizer strips our land of its nutrients and pollutes our waterways, third, it contributes to climate change, and lastly industrial fertilization of crops promotes monocultures and poor land management. Now, at a crossroads where petroleum products are being intensely guarded by their host nations and supply is being artificially restricted, even as we face a once-in-history crisis of the climate, our agricultural system is threatened with collapse, and even famine.

Have you noticed that lettuce has been in short supply in recent months and years? Grocery store shelves are empty. When there is lettuce, prices are higher than ever before.

Maryland

In 2021, shortages in the chemical *urea* led to inefficiencies creating nitrogen based fertilizer, and plants shut down around the world from China to the UK to the United States. Further, China restricted exports of fertilizer, threatening food production worldwide. As a result, prices for nitrogen fertilizer have sky-rocketed. "Global prices of nitrogen in November exceeded $1,000 per tonne for the first time ever," according to *Food Business News*. "Disruptions in countries that are major fertilizer producers, such as Belarus for potash and China for phosphate and nitrogen, affect the global fertilizer supply chain even if they are not major suppliers to the United States,"Corey Rosenbusch of The Fertilizer Institute said. "China, which accounts for about a third of the global supply of urea nitrogen fertilizer, has banned phosphate and urea exports until June 2022 after reducing or stopping production to conserve electricity."

Where does that leave us? In the United States, sixty nine percent of cropland is treated with nitrogen-based fertilizer. That nets to over six-hundred-thirty million acres of farmland treated yearly, from corn in Iowa to lettuce in California. The United States is one of the largest food exporters in the world, and is self-sufficient when it comes to food production and the ability to feed the population, but if our food production falls, this self-sufficiency will be threatened.

Let me take you through the numbers. America exports twenty five percent of farm products annually, and according to agronomic researchers at Mosaic, crop yields would decline by forty percent without nitrogen fertilizer. This would be true in other countries, too, which would stop exporting produce to the United States. Combined, this would have a devastating effect on food availability, because our nation imports approximately fifteen percent of our food to meet demand.

Laying this out, say Americans collectively produce 100 units of food, 40 of which are dependent on fertilizer and 25 of which are exported. America demands 90 units of food, so we import 15 units from other countries to meet demand. In a functioning world, the equation looks like this:

SUPPLY: 100 - 25 + 15 = 90 **:DEMAND**

The equation balances. Now, say the world runs into a fertilizer shortage. The most likely scenario would be a reduction, rather than an elimination, of that supply. Say we reduce our fertilizer-dependent units from 40 to 20. This will occur worldwide, and where it doesn't occur, those countries will protect their crops fastidiously. There will be no food to import, and we will restrict exports. The equation now looks like this.

SUPPLY: 80 - 0 + 0 ≠ 90 **:DEMAND**

Here, we have a food deficit of 10 units. People will go hungry, and this isn't even a worst-case scenario. In the short run, the American government will release reserve food supplies like cheese, wheat, and beef. It will release oil reserves and loosen restrictions on fossil fuel manufacturing to boost fertilizer production. In the short term, nothing will look out of sorts. In the long run, however, reserves will run out, austerity will be called for, and home-production of fertilizers will become unsustainable. In a plausible scenario, crop yields will be reduced to a fully unfertilized level, and the equation will look like this.

$$\textbf{SUPPLY: } 60 - 0 + 0 \neq 90 \textbf{ :DEMAND}$$

More will starve than before. We may switch back to cow manure, but cows eat grains, and we will have to restrict the production of beef, and thus cow manure. Monoculture crops which rely on chemical fertilizers and pesticides to stay alive, unable to sustain themselves, may fall further. Optimistically, we may turn to smaller farmers and local growers, perhaps even growing our own gardens in a widespread national movement. Perhaps this adds 5 units of food to our supply, which traditional agriculture falls further. Lack of grain drives down beef and grain-fed poultry, costing us 15 units of food (chicken and beef are the top consumed meats in the United States). Crop failure costs us another 10 units of food. A dire equation now looks like this:

$$\textbf{SUPPLY: } 35 + 5 \text{ (small farms)} - 0 + 0 \neq 90 \textbf{ :DEMAND}$$

In this scenario, a waterfall effect caused by the restriction of fertilizers *now* and the inability to shift the global supply chain away from fossil fuels, the majority of Americans starve. This is famine.

And this is not some wildcard prediction. Humanitarian workers and NGO operators worldwide are warning of a looming hunger crisis. Today, forty-five percent of deaths among children under five are caused by hunger.

Mike Bonke of Action Against Hunger puts it bluntly: "In over 15 years working in the aid sector, I can't remember the humanitarian situation looking so bleak. The threat of famine looms large in several countries and yet it feels like world leaders are watching from the stands."

Further, as I illustrated, this isn't an *other people in another country are starving* problem. It's an American problem. *Bloomberg* notes that "According to the charity Feeding America, the number of people needing food assistance soared to 60 million in 2020, up 50% from the previous year," and "only thanks to emergency federal intervention was a serious hunger crisis averted in 2020."

These are startling figures. If it's hard to imagine an America without food, look around you. We've discussed the logistics crisis and staffing shortages in retailers, but that isn't the root of the crisis in food supply. It comes down to production. Simply, America isn't able to produce enough to eat. The question remains, *What do we do now?*

Our Imperative

Our imperative facing a collapsing food system is multifold: personal, local, and political. The personal imperatives are the easiest. If you can, grow *something*, even if it's not a full garden. Understand the seasonality of crops and grow winter kale, summer square, and spring beans. Commit to growing food for your family, and what you can't grow, commit to buying as locally as possible. These are personal imperatives. To aid you in achieving these goals, joining them with local imperatives. If your community doesn't have a CSA, form one with a local farm and use the power of numbers to provide your local growers with the customers necessary to sustain themselves. Go to local farmers associations and advocate for organic and biodynamic growing, and work with your local schools, churches, and businesses to drive business to regional farmers. Not only will your lettuce, milk, corn and so much more taste better, but community life will improve, too. You and your neighbors will have developed shared goals, networks, and political capital. You will have developed power. Agriculture and community sit at the base of all political power – church power, monarchical power, and yes, democratic power – and to seize control of that power through *literal* grass-roots organizing will give you and your community the strength to make this fight political. It will take time, but when the community *is* the economy and *is* the provider of jobs and *is* the control center of capital, representatives in our republic will pay attention. You will have a machine powerful enough to swing elections, all built on common commitment to wholesome food, good jobs, and stable communities. Political imperatives addressing fossil fuel usage, monocultures, and big agriculture can come from an informed, engaged community heart, and spread good practices and democratic strength to every American hearth. This is our imperative. This is how we find *hope* instead of famine.

ECOSYSTEMIC COLLAPSE

Consumers, at least if they're not living in poverty, have an enormous role to play, too. If you don't like the way the business does its business, don't buy their products. This is beginning to create change. People should think about the consequences of the little choices they make each day.

– JANE GOODALL

There are only 67 Javan rhinoceroses left in the wild. Mountain gorillas, tigers, and elephants are nearing extinction, too. When we imagine a future of technological advancement, tranquility, and prosperity, we must also think of a future so inhospitable to animals, and even many plants, that the sapiosphere is truly complete.

Unpredictable rains have washed away towns in Germany and America, fields of crops in India and Bangladesh, vineyards in France, and habitats across the world in the past year. Fires burn in evergreen forests in Canada, Washington, and Russia. Mountains are leveled by mining machinery, and cities are leveled by hurricanes and typhoons. What are we supposed to do?

In 2020, *The New York Times* released an interactive report showing that no county in the United States would go unaffected by sea level rise, water stress, fires, hurricanes, excess rainfall and flooding, or heat stress. The wealthiest and the poorest areas alike would suffer *somehow* under the effects of climate change. And yet we are not hopeless.

Right now, even if you aren't feeling the effects of climate change in your day-to-day weather, you are feeling it in the supply chain. "As climate change makes extreme weather more frequent and/ or severe, it increases the annual probability of events that are more intense than manufacturing assets are constructed to withstand, increasing the likelihood of supply-chain disruptions," global consulting firm McKinsey writes. What this means, really, is that climate issues are at the root of the other problems we've already covered. "It's obvious that the impacts of climate change that we're already experiencing today, wildfires, drought, extreme weather, more intense hurricanes, crop yield declines, water shortage and the political disruption that comes from the forced migration and political instability it generates — these are enormous stress to many supply chains of companies, and not just companies that are making physical products but in finance and services," John Sterman, a professor at MIT, told CNBC last year.

Actual extreme weather events like fires disrupt shipping, and hurricanes disrupt ports. Desertification makes it harder to grow crops, feed the working populace, and staff factories. Migration from water and heat stress reduces nations' labor capabilities, and stresses manufacturers, shippers, and more throughout the economy. Change and a new path forward begin here at home. While yes, corporations and governments are responsible for the vast majority of damage to the world, that does not leave us powerless. I described a method of turning local economy and agriculture into political power, and much the same model could be put to work here, too.

Climate change isn't *good* for society. We know this. Here we'll discuss two very important examples of *how* climate change is damaging our economy and society, however: labor and food production. We've discussed previously how both threaten our way of life – labor shortages threaten our logistics and retail infrastructures, and falling food production threatens to plunge us into famine – add climate change to the mix, on top of greedy employers and geopolitical fertilizer wars, and we have a three-headed-dog at the gates to our American hellscape.

Climate Change Is Changing Labor

McKinsey is only speaking of *disaster* impacts here, but the breakdown of effects climate crises can have on supply chains and industry is telling

> *There are three drivers of near-term losses for suppliers that are hit by such events, potentially leading to losses of up to 200 percent of annual profit and 35 percent of revenues: physical damages to assets, including facilities, production equipment, and inventories; reduced sales, either because production is disrupted or because goods cannot be shipped to the market; and higher costs in the reconstruction phase and after the plant is back in production, as market prices of labor, energy, and logistics may spike following a disaster.*

But how does climate change affect the labor force? According to *The Lancet*, "current climate conditions already negatively affect labour effectiveness, particularly in tropical countries," and this will only increase in years to come. Heat and water stress decrease productivity of those who work outdoors, such a field laborers in our agriculture system, and these same forces push people to migrate to less-impacted regions, increasing the costs of labor by restricting supply. Further, pollution, heat, and other air quality issues impact services and indoor workers, too. More heat means more air conditioning, meaning more electricity usage and pollution. Higher rates of particulate matter in the air are notably linked to decreases in our productivity. Combined, we see that climate change, and particularly the outphased term *global warming*, hits our economy from a number of directions.

As we produce less food or the prices of food rise with labor costs passed on the consumer, people have a harder time getting what they need to eat and survive. Increased migration stresses our political systems, threatening to destabilize whole nations, as has begun to happen in Central America, the United States, Turkey, and Italy in particular. Air quality effects on services, intellectual industries, and other office workers means our logistics and finance infrastructure is slower to respond, as work is getting done less efficiently. Each person has more to worry about closer to home, crises of increased food costs, electricity bills, and even brain fog on the job or illness caused by pollution in the air.

Even if we're not facing disruptions from forest fires every day or everywhere, the global economy, interconnected as it is today, shipping upwards of twenty trillion dollars of trade each year, is suffering a labor crisis brought on by climate change and increased heat stress.

Climate Change Is Lowering Crop Yields

According to NASA, "average global crop yields for corn may see a decrease of 24% by late century, with the declines becoming apparent by 2030." Food, along with everything else, is profoundly impacted by the climate. Growing conditions changing even slightly means flooding, blight, a new dust bowl, or heat death for many different types of crops. "Whether you're in the agricultural sector or the forestry sector, or in the tech sector, there is really no particular sector that is immune from climate change," said

Charles Slay of the Sustainability Consortium.

By the end of the decade, we could be looking at a very different world in terms of *what there is to eat. National Geographic* predicts declines of -24% for corn, -3% for wheat, -11% for rice, and -9% for potatoes, the four staple starches eaten around the world and used across a plethora of industries and products. Corn isn't just used as *corn on the cob*, but is essential for the production of ethanol, is used as cattle and poultry feed, and is the basis of corn syrup, which is used as a sweetener in many processed foods.

Can we live without corn syrup and with less beef? Yes, but our world is currently built around these crops, and while we *can* live without as much of them, disruptions of this sort will be massive shocks to the system, causing discontent, anxiety, and temporary hunger in many places. We will be forced to more seriously address food waste, and as we discussed before, faced with the choice of rebuilding regional economies or starving.

And regional growing may not always be an option: rice is the most eaten grain in the world, and *National Geographic* reports that "changes in Asia, with its large population and land area, will affect the most people. India and China will experience major losses of arable land." It will be difficult for many Asians to build local agronomies around rice and other crops, just as it will be difficult for North and South Americans, Australians, Europeans, and Africans... in short, it will be difficult for everyone. In South America, "crops will suffer... and corn farmers will see crops decline by nearly 16 percent," while in Europe "potato farmers will see longer growing seasons. Fields farther south will become increasingly dry."

Disruptions in growing will strike a blow to the heart of our economy and our society, so we must prepare - not in the *doomsday-prepper-in-a-bunker* sort of way, but in a wholesome, balanced, community-minded sort of way.

Our Imperative

We have found imperatives in labor and food production already. Now we add the lens of climate change and find ourselves a clearer imperative than before. Again there are imperatives for all levels of society, from the individual to the sociopolitical engines of state. Personally, we must *recommit to doing no harm*, and where we *do* harm, which we undoubtedly will do, we must recommit to correcting that harm. Build for ourselves where we can, do without where we can, and *want less*. Be someone who requires less luxury and leaves less of a footprint on society and the earth.

I do not need to tell you *how* to do this – there is enough literature about reducing waste, buying less, composting more, and the list goes on – no, I'm here to tell you that you *must* do this. You *must* live change. Living change will guide your relationships with the community. You will run on the streets instead of burning fossil fuels to run on a treadmill, and perhaps you will find someone to run with.

At the local level, talk to your small businesses about the importance of being green - and how doing so can save them money. Buying locally may mean they rely less on expensive foreign ingredients, or that they can get things fresher, relying less on expensive refrigeration costs. They will have more money to hire people, and retail people with better wages, so people will not need to travel as far for work, burning fuel in a commute. These are small changes. But our imperative is to make these changes *large*. Make these changes *political*, and give a wholesome life your whole voice and your whole body. Mend your clothes. Grow herbs. Walk more. Wake with the sun and sleep with the night. Buy no plastic. Plant a tree. Live for your *community* and *live for yourself.*

You think, is this communist, or is this libertarian? Can it be neither? I'll tell you - it's green, it's human, it's wholesome, and it's anti-corporate. Life can be free, fulfilling, and full of joy and be neither adherent to libertarian nihilism or communist optimism. Freedom is to be found in perfecting the small choices and leaving the world better than we found it. Horrors will still occur, and oppression will still be a crisis, but we can live simply, be humble, be wholesome, and find peace in our imperative for a better life.

Hope for emerging from a hellscape of our own design is found within. It is found at home.

Return to the Jane Goodall quote I began this section with: "Consumers, at least if they're not living in poverty, have an enormous role to play, too. If you don't like the way the business does its business, don't buy their products. This is beginning to create change. People should think about the consequences of the little choices they make each day"

EMERGING FROM HELL

Strideth over all mountains, and laugheth at all tragedies

– FRIEDRICH NIETSCHE

I asked you What can you do? Is there hope? How can you plan a life and achieve happiness?

I hope, if you've read this little book in completeness, that you now know *what to do*. You must seize power in your everyday life and deliver it to yourself and your community. You must encourage every home to be a crucible of change, and every business to become wholesome rather than sociopathic. As a modern society we face something unprecedented. Emerging from a pandemic where we failed to make any noticeable changes to our way of life and solve systemic problems like worker abuse and climate change, events like the *Ever Given* give us comedy from the tragedy.

Our tragedy is a crisis of economics which will disrupt the lives of millions throughout the world in the years to come. Terrible working conditions will push families to the brink and destroy relationships, lives, and communities. Monocultures and reliance on fossil fertilizers in our food system will drive us to famine, crop loss, and disease. Rising costs for materials will make modern life that much more inaccessible to the poor. And climate change will make life hotter, harder, and drier, eliminating livable green spaces, especially for urban dwellers, people of color, and the poor, leading to political discontent and instability, mental health crises, and lower productivity and engagement in society.

Finding hope among this chaos is possible but difficult. If we want to give our children something greater, then we must not be complacent. Facing a crisis of political origin, remember George Orwell, the journalist and author who said "Political language... is designed to make lies sound truthful and murder respectable, and to give an appearance of solidity to pure wind." Face politics with local power. Retake our democracy with *roots of oak* not *roots of grass*. When we rebuild, today and tomorrow, from the death and waste around us, do we want a new order to endure? Do we want principles of biodynamics, community, and dignity to endure? Or do you want to leave this fight to your children, as your parents did for you?

Are you left wondering *what should I do?* Have I not been clear enough for you? I'll put it more bluntly: to save the world and rebuild thriving communities *you must make impactful decisions and have difficult conversations.* You must make yourself an agent of power, and a player in the outcome. An impactful choice isn't whether to buy loose lettuce or boxed. It is whether to organize a plastic packaging boycott in your town of forty thousand and make all the boxed lettuce on the shelves wilt. You must have courage and endurance, because the latter choice isn't easy – it is hard to take it upon yourself to lead and be change, but that is what the oppressor is counting on. They are counting on your fear, your inexperience, and your apathy. Do not give it to them.

An impactful choice is forcing the hand of those stronger than you by marshaling the forces of the people with better skill than they. Organize. Act. Endure. This is how to save the world and rebuild thriving communities.

ABOUT THE AUTHOR

Douglas Vogel

 Vogel is an American thinker, writer, and author. He is a community organizer and libertarian communist. He grew up in Maine and now lives in the Bronx with his wife and German shepherd, Hank.

He urges readers to make changes in their lives and communities that they can be proud of.